The Ma of Chaos Magick

Practical Techniques For Directing Your Reality

Adam Blackthorne

Copyright © 2016 Adam Blackthorne

All Rights Reserved. This book may not be reproduced, in whole or in part, in any form or by any means electronic or mechanical, including photocopying, recording, or by any information storage retrieval system now known or hereafter invented, without written permission from the publisher, The Gallery of Magick.

It is hereby expressly stated that the images in this book may not be reproduced in any form, except for individual and personal use. Derivative works based on these images or the associated concepts are not permitted, and any such attempt to create a derivative work will be met with legal action.

Disclaimer: Consider all information in this book to be speculation and not professional advice, to be used at your own risk. Adam Blackthorne and The Gallery of Magick are not responsible for the consequences of your actions. The information is never intended to replace or substitute for financial or medical advice from a professional advisor, and when it comes to matters of finance or health you should always seek conventional, professional advice. The information is provided on the understanding that you will use it in accordance with the laws of your country.

CONTENTS

Chapter 1: Make Magick Happen — 7

Chapter 2: The First Step — 15

Chapter 3: Instant Alchemy — 19

Chapter 4: The Core of Desire — 23

Chapter 5: Emotional Crafting — 27

Chapter 6: The Fire of Gnosis — 35

Chapter 7: Magickal Chaos Energy — 43

Chapter 8: Influence Magick — 47

Chapter 9: Thoughtforms and The Other People — 53

Chapter 10: Upside Down Sex Magick — 59

Chapter 11: Contacting Spirits — 61

Chapter 12: Olympic Chaos Magick — 65

Chapter 13: Making New Magick — 89

Chapter 14: The Magick of Pure Invention — 95

Chapter 15: The Big Picture — 97

Afterword — 99

Chapter 1: Make Magick Happen

This book will provide you with magick you can actually use. I might get everything else wrong, but I promise you this: the heart of this book is magick that works.

Chaos Magick is meant to be the most practical, simplified, bare-bones way to shift reality in a way that agrees with your desire and your true will. There's a bizarre irony that most books on Chaos Magick give you wild theory, but no practical magick. I'll do what I can to set things right on that front. There's nothing quite like doing magick and seeing it work, so that's what lies ahead of you.

Chaos Magick is not about causing chaos with magick. It's about reordering your reality and directing life the way you want. Just like normal magick, but without a lot of the frills. It's not quite as exacting and formulaic as old-fashioned magick, so maybe that's why it was called 'chaos.' When it was invented, it probably seemed like a great big sloppy madness compared to the refined rites, robes, and rituals of old. Even though it works.

There are millions of approximate definitions, but if you asked me for a definition right now, I'd say that Chaos Magick is an occult technology that puts an emphasis on simplification, flexible beliefs, emotional transmutation, and results. If it doesn't work, it isn't magick.

Chaos Magick sounds like it might be a slapdash magick for lazy unbelievers. But it works. If you have imagination, it works. If you are good at pretending, it works. If you can be playful, it works. If you can access your feelings, it works. If you have willpower, it works. If you combine all these things, you'll be crowned Grand Magus of Chaos Magick within a week.

And yes, it can be slapdash. You can cobble together a ritual and see the magick work. It works better than half the rubbish you find in those very thick, heavy dusty tomes that fill a particular shelf of The British Library. But you will get better results if you're a bit more thorough. And here's a big secret, straight away, in the sixth paragraph, a great big secret: being thorough doesn't mean having the right tools and wands and words and sigils – it means letting your emotions drive your magick. And I can show you exactly how to do that.

Let's pause for a moment. Magick is serious. What you experience is real; it affects your reality. It's not a joke, and the spiritual development you undergo is absolute. But it can get so pretentious that you lose sight of the fact that magick is really about finding joy in your universe, and reshaping the very universe itself to give you more joy. Let's not be too pompous.

If I'm lighthearted at times, that doesn't mean I'm treating magick frivolously. I'm just keeping my mind open and as supple as I can manage at my age. An open mind is how you make magick work because an open mind makes way for the energy of emotion. And, when you do one little ritual and see one big, surprising, honey-dripping result, you're going to feel a jolt of joy. You'll probably laugh, even while sensing a whopping, heavy, somber awareness of your own power. Magick's like that. Full of contradictions. But, let's try to keep our focus on magick that works.

I'm not going to bore you with economic theory, quantum physics or my personal philosophy regarding the nature of reality. When people write about Chaos Magick, they go off on weird non-magickal tangents and write about all sorts of utterly non-magickal ideas they've had. This is fun for the writers but is less effective for you than throwing a coin in a well and making a wish. (Actually, wishing wells can work – but you need to add a little magickal twist. More on that later.)

Chaos Magick is still a developing art, but its heyday was in the eighties and nineties. There were some good books written and some great occultists who introduced core ideas. It started in the seventies when nobody was paying much attention. At that time, a lot of the magick was developed by kids - teenagers with attitude who wanted to get magick working, even though they didn't have access to the inner sanctum of traditional occultism. They read the basic ideas and ran with them. Imaginative kids with ideas bigger than their fears. They made magick new.

It's a horrible irony that most of the Chaos Magick books written today are as dogmatic, wordy and downright dull as the ancient tomes they used to scorn. Listening to somebody talk about Chaos Magick can be like going to a really tedious Catholic Sermon. You want to ask the priest how to make prayers actually work, but he keeps talking about sin. In Latin.

Theory can be thought-provoking, but it doesn't get things done. There are many Chaos Magick books that explain how it all works – even though nobody really knows how it works. What I know is that it does work. If you want to get into magick, this is a fast and reasonably easy way. If you've been using magick for years, I hope you'll get into the shortcuts and simplifications to keep magick efficient and effective.

Magick is a noble, spiritual, wonderful art that can help you learn about reality and yourself, but it's also a great way to get more money, look after your love life, and influence the thoughts and feelings of others. If you've got a moral problem with that, then mayhap you don't want to dabble with magick. But if you're worried about affecting other people, you might have to lock yourself in your cellar. You already affect and influence people, and you even control them with your stern words, pretty smiles, wise frowns and harsh wishes. Every hope, every promise, every request, every action you make has an influence. Which means that magick won't make you evil, it just makes it easier to get things done. If you're a good person, you won't be evil. Sounds obvious when you write it down, but people miss the point oh so easily.

Magick makes your intentions much more real. If you have an intention, it can manifest. That is power. Make sure you're ready to have this much fun and this much power. It can change your life.

For every chaos magician who prospers, there are plenty who are still hammering out mini-rituals every day to make a few extra pennies. It's not always spectacular. I'll do my level best to show you what works, what doesn't, and where it all goes wrong, so you can make sure it usually goes right.

If you've seen other books by The Gallery of Magick, you might wonder why on earth we're publishing a book about Chaos Magick. If you believe everything you hear, then you'll believe that Chaos Magick is all about making stuff up, pretending to believe and hacking the universe, with no respect for angels, demons or anything else. And yet, books by The Gallery of Magick are about *real* angels, spirits, and entities that can assist your life. So what's the truth?

First of all, Chaos Magick is *not* just about making things up. Yes, you can invent a ritual and get it to work, and yes, Chaos Magick can be about taking bits from one system and pieces from another. But, at its best, this magick is about personal exploration and having a deep connection to the reality of magick itself.

The Gallery of Magick, as a magickal order, have always simplified things. If you get hold of a copy of *The 72 Angels of Magick*, it might look like a complex system of chants, sigils, and psychological shifting. But compared to tradition, it is a massive, outrageous simplification. According to occult theory and tradition, it shouldn't work. But it damn well does.

One thing we've dedicated ourselves to is exactly that. Simplification. That is what we learned from Chaos Magick – the ability to throw out the wands and daggers and magick circles, and the extra fluff and junk that you don't need. Magick can work when the essence is all that's left. That's what you already get in books by The Gallery of Magick. It isn't Chaos Magick, but it's been informed by the revolution of Chaos. It's the essence of traditional magick, and I don't for one minute reject it. Use that magick, but use Chaos Magick too, because Chaos can be highly flexible, intuitive, impromptu and adapted to your exact needs.

But just wait a minute. Those other books are about contacting angels and other spirits. Are the spirits real? Does it matter? To me, the spirits are absolutely real. I have seen too much to think otherwise. Call me crazy, but I've spoken to angels (and I wasn't on drugs), and I believe they are real. But you don't need to believe in them. It's possible I conjured them up through imagination. Think that, if it helps. Believe or don't believe, because it won't change a thing. Belief is a tool in Chaos Magick, so faith is not a ticket to success. If you believe that angels are only as real as unicorns, the magick can still work.

You can get magick to work so long as you believe in magick. That's all you need. You don't need to believe in particular gods, angels, demons or spirits. Just know that magick is real. Believe that the mind can affect the universe in a supernatural way.

You already know that the mind can affect reality. You think about moving your hand and your hand moves. A thought has directed matter to shift. Not an original example, I know, but it's a good one. The ephemeral mind can make matter move, and that's remarkable. We reside in bodies that can determine how we feel (when we get sick, tired, injured), but we can also direct our bodies to move, create, or jump around the room. Thoughts move bodies, bodies build stuff, and life goes on. It's weird. Magick only requires a tiny leap of faith to know that your mind, your will, your emotions and your intent can affect reality beyond the confines of your nerves and bones. If you're reading this book, it's probably because you already believe that magick is a reality.

You can make up reasons to believe it's all true. This is what most Chaos Magick books help you with – they talk about the way the mind exists in a moment of quantum flux and a string of multiverse potential. That sort of stuff. It sounds scientific and exciting, but it's really just gobbledygook to convince you that the reality of magick is backed up by science. Most scientists would laugh you out of the room if they read it; better to just trust your hunch about magick.

If you believe the universe is just nuts and bolts working in a mechanical way, please put your skills to use in engineering. We need good engineers. But if you sense that there's some level of supernatural in the world, if you think your human mind can be a part of that, if you get the slightest hunch that this might be true, you can get magick to work.

When I was a kid, I was completely freaked out by the number of religions that were for sale. I lived in a town that was multicultural, and I just found it so weird that somebody could choose one religion when right next door there were other religions on offer. How could you pick a belief and really believe it when right next door there was so much faith that went in a completely different direction? And then, when I got into magick, I felt the same way. There are lots of different systems, all with their own sets of beliefs. How do you know which one is the true magick? Well, you don't, so you can just try bits of magick from all of them. And then you find that they *all* work. The answer is that magick itself works. The flavor of magick is not so important.

If magick has been used by a lot of people, a lot of times, then it's more likely to work. To ignore those traditions would be to ignore a lot of good magickal technology. In Chaos Magick you use what works, regardless of origin. Your world changes.

Modern occultists can be so efficient. You read the old books, and you're told you have to hack a particular tree to bits on a particular day, in order to make a wand. Oh yeah? I used a wand that I stole out of my brother's magick trick box set that he got for Christmas. It worked. You can even use your finger instead of a wand. Or your foot. It's the act of pointing that counts, not what the stick is made out of. My wand was plastic, and it worked for me. My toes work as well. When you point a wand (or your foot), you're making a grand gesture. Chaos Magick cares about the gestures, not the tools so much. The stick itself isn't important.

Traditional magick is fascinating to some, including me. Like my colleagues, I love reading old books, working my way through piles of old documents, searching for a tiny insight into ancient magick, or a secret sigil that the world may have missed. But that's a hobby. Practical magick can be so simple that you spend a couple of minutes doing a ritual, and it works. You think of something you want, you create the magick to get the result, and the result happens. Those bumper stickers that say *Magic Happens*…they really should say *Chaos Magick Happens*. Because it does.

Chapter 2: The First Step

People say that Chaos Magick is about taking on a belief, using it for a while, and then discarding it. That's sort of true, but this creates the impression that we're just pretending one thing after another. It's a bit more sophisticated than that. I think the best way to approach chaos magick is to accept that all magick can work. It's all real.

Some chaos magicians say that even fictional magick works. If you do spells from *Harry Potter* or use The Force from *Star Wars*, you can supposedly get results. That's what some people think, but I'm not a big fan of that approach because it feels too silly, and it automatically connects you to a feeling of fiction. Things being made up. Not real. And not getting results. If you disagree with me, well, there's room for all ideas in Chaos. We invent, reinvent and change as we go, and nobody owns this magick. If you want to use fiction instead of more established methods, you can adapt everything I say by putting in a bit of made-up magick. This book will focus on spirits and methods that some people regard as real because that's going to charge up your magick a bit faster.

I think a mistake people make is to think that if you pretend to believe something, you're doing Chaos Magick, and that's the end of it. Making things up is not as powerful as taking a belief that already exists. If other people have genuinely believed in a power, that power can work for you. Pretending to use a spell from Harry Potter won't work so well, because nobody really believes in Harry Potter as a reality. Everybody knows it's fiction. But, use a bit of angelic Hebrew magick, and you're tapping into a real belief system.

The belief does not need to be global. If seventeen people genuinely believe in the power of The Wild Hog of Grizedale, you could invoke that beast and use its power. The sincerity of the belief is the bit that matters.

In Chaos Magick, people have been borrowing beliefs for decades, so this secret is not big news. But, I think it's a real time-saver to focus on the established beliefs of others, and archetypal energies, to get the magick going. You can make up magick, you can invent entities (and you will do some of that in this book), but when you want to access the most fertile energies of creation, the pathway to that power is the belief of others. You don't need to believe what somebody else believes, you only need to act as though you have that belief. Speak to an angel as though it's real and the angel will help you whether you believe or not.

You still get to make magick up from scratch once you're in tune with the energies at hand. It can be very creative. Making magick your own is a big part of all this. But, when you need a quick jolt of real magick, you can dip your finger into anything from hoodoo to pagan rites, and the pressure of belief behind the magick will bring you results.

If you believe that magick is a reality, you're going to be ok. You can get magick underway, and as you go, you'll find that you *do* believe. It becomes really, really obvious that magick just works.

In many of the old, established magickal orders, Initiation was the first step to magick. It still goes on today, and it's a long, slow, and often expensive process. There are usually a lot of old people (usually men) making you feel inferior, teaching you some very boring and largely fruitless rituals, and then eventually telling you you're initiated, and then they follow that up by saying that you can't really do much, and you're going to have to wait a lot longer, and spend more money, and take more instruction, before you can do any magick that works. What I love about Chaos Magick is that people who read about sigil magick go out and make a sigil, and get a magickal result *that week*, making the old orders look a bit stuffy. Doing magick - *that* is initiation.

You really don't need a room full of old men to initiate you; you just need to do some magick. The moment you get one magickal result, that's it, done, you're a magician. You've been initiated. And then when you make up some magick of your own and get it to work, you can give yourself some grand title and start your own magickal order. Or, if you're a sensible person, forget all that posturing and just do magick that works to get a better life.

My next sentence should be something telling you that it's time to do some magick. Nearly, almost – we're nearly there, but not quite. This is where a lot of people stumble with Chaos Magick. They get to this point, all excited, and think, 'Ok, let's give it a test drive and see if it works.'

No, no, no! When you take a car for a test drive, you do not do so to see if it works. You know it works. Cars work. That car better *had* work because it's sitting in a showroom, pristine and polished and with one purpose – to be driven. You test drive a car not to see if it works, but to see how it feels, how much you want it, what it can do for you. When you go into magick, you should not think of it as a test of the magick's veracity. If you do, the magick will turn on you like a trodden weasel, or it will just fizzle out to meet your expectations of failure.

This is not an experiment. OK, it's true, lots of magick *is* about experimentation and trying things out and seeing what works, and genuinely giving yourself feedback on what's useful and what isn't. No point in keeping a crappy spell that doesn't work. But, when you set out, you should do so with a commitment to magick. If you test the magick, it's like you're saying, 'OK magick, I'm pretty special and know all about reality, so let's see if you can meet my expectations and live up to my high standards.' It's a bit arrogant and entitled. Magick works, and you should just treat it as real rather than seeing if it can appease your skepticism.

Now, this doesn't mean you have to bow down respectfully before magick. Not one bit of that. But, you do need to treat it as though it's real. Can you imagine if you went down to that showroom to test drive a car, and you're sitting there going, 'OK, well let's see if turning this key really does fire up the combustion engine that will make these wheels turn. Oh, wow, the engine started. I don't believe it.' You'd look a bit foolish. You turn the key because you know the engine will fire (Unless there's a fault.)

That's how you approach magick. There probably isn't a fault with the engine. Turn the key, because you know it will fire up. Perform the ritual, because you know magick works. (I stole that example from a good friend of mine – because that's how he convinced me to believe in magick. Turn the key!)

Decide now that you're going to do magick, as part of your life, because it works. Take it into your life as a reality. You will experiment, and you will find what works best for you, but experimentation in Chaos Magick means trying new things with courage and expectation, rather than measuring and testing as accurately as a scientist. You're going to get a pretty clear idea of what works best for you, without focusing on judgment. After a few weeks you might love sigil magick, or you might not. It will be really clear that it works for you, or that it's a bit of a letdown. No need to test it and evaluate it. You'll just know. Now, let's do some magick.

Chapter 3: Instant Alchemy

We're going to do some magick. And the key to magick is not faith, belief, a good collection of herbs, or anything like that. It's emotion. There are a lot of other tools that we can use such as special words, archetypal images and various states of mind, but the engine of magick is emotion.

A lot of folks get their magick to work, and never know that it worked because their emotions shifted in a particularly magickal way. They might do another ritual and get no results, not realizing that it's all because the emotional component was missing. When you know about the role of emotion in magick, you really have found a hack that can make just about any magick work.

Messing about with your emotions like this is really easy, and it changes the world. It doesn't just change you; it makes actual physical things happen. All those things you read about on the back of magick books. Money, love, influence, power. When you put emotion into your magick, it can do all these things.

This is even true with more traditional magick. If you call to an angel and ask for help, guess how you direct the angel. With emotion. Guess what makes the angel respond best to your needs. Emotion. Whether you're using traditional magick to contact real entities that you believe in or just going through the magickal motions because you want a result, it's the emotions that *you* change during the ritual that create your result.

This is alchemy. You take one feeling and turn it into another. Reality then gets modified to meet your emotions.

I could just end the book here because you know it all now, but I'll add some details as we go. But, keep this in mind for the rest of your career in Chaos.

We'll start with the easiest magick of all. It's called sigil magick; you've probably heard about it before, and maybe even been bored to death by reading the same old dull descriptions. Here we go. This is traditional sigil magick. You write down your request, turn that sentence into a bunch of squiggles and then fire that squiggle off into the universe using some sort of altered consciousness.

There are thousands of websites describing the process, but let me have a go at showing you how to do it better than most people. Sigil magick has such great potential but is usually disappointing. Let's turn that around. This is Sigil Magick Remastered.

The traditional Chaos Magick approach starts out by having you write down your desire as a positive statement. Instead of saying, 'I don't want to be poor,' you say, 'I want to be rich,' and then you shift that to the present tense. 'I am rich.' The trouble with this is that it doesn't sound at all convincing. You know you're not rich, and it just feels wrong to pretend that you are. It's like those affirmations that people use in an attempt to change their personality. 'I am a confident and loving person.' It sounds so fake. I detest affirmations because I think they stimulate and generate the opposite emotion, and then they make that unpleasant emotion grow. Even if you are a fairly confident person, repeating the affirmation 'I am confident' can lead you to feel more insecure, no matter how often you repeat that mantra to yourself. And that's one big problem with the traditional approach to sigil magick.

It feels weird to talk about traditional Chaos Magick because it's meant to be radical and new, but the truth is it's become a bit traditional. And I think that the traditional approach to sigilisation is dead in the water. Yeah, it can work, it has worked, and it's not all bad, but let's try something new and better.

The Gallery of Magick developed an approach to sigil magick that's a bit more inventive. This wasn't my idea, so I feel ok about going on about how great it is. I *love* this technique. All you do is phrase the result as a question about something that once happened. This ever-so-subtle shift transforms the magick.

If you want to find the money to buy a new piano, you'd write, 'How did I come to own this beautiful piano?'

It's a question that you never attempt to answer.

It's a question that assumes the result has already come about.

It's a question that acknowledges the sense of wonder and appreciation you feel at having this result.

The universe will answer the question by changing reality to match the emotion of the question.

You are sort of pretending that, in this very moment, you've achieved your goal, and you're pondering the wonder of the result with a pleasant appreciation. You're *not* trying to answer the question.

Have you ever found yourself in some amazing city, or with an amazing person, and you go, 'How the hell did I end up here?' The feeling is something along the lines of, 'This is so wonderful. Wow.' That's a good place to be, feeling wonderful and looking back with pleasant incredulity. You're not for a moment trying to answer the question. You ask the question just to express joy. Put that in your magick, and your magick will work.

In the next chapter, we'll look at how to create and refine this question. The chapter might take a few minutes to read, but the technique itself only takes a few seconds once you get the hang of it.

Chapter 4: The Core of Desire

Before you create a sigil, job number one is to find a target – a result you want, something that could actually change without it being a crazy unbelievable miracle. It should be something that's not likely to happen without magick, but it shouldn't be something outrageously difficult. Not at first.

When you apply magick to an area of your life that *could* change, magick will make that little push for you. Let's say you want to buy that piano. Be creative and look at all the ways you could get the piano, and work out which ones feel good. What you probably don't want is for magick to give you some extra overtime at work in an effort to give you the extra money. That would feel bad. You probably also don't want a loan or an increase in your credit limit. That would feel fake. You want to pay for that piano and take it home feeling like it's truly yours. Ok, so that's the emotion you need to focus on. You don't worry one bit about where the money's going to come from, or how you're going to get it. But you think about how you want to feel when you get it. You concern yourself with the *satisfaction* of getting the piano in a way that feels good to you. Think about how that would feel.

Don't become a problem solver. You're not directing the magick or telling it where to get the money. You're working out what result would feel good. Getting some overtime would not feel good. Paying with an increased credit limit would not feel good. But, handing over a wad of cash and feeling like you really own the piano – that feels good. Seeing it delivered to your door, fully paid off… that feels good.

You are categorically *not* trying to solve the problem of where the money comes from. You're just feeling your way around the result to make sure you find one that *feels right*. Doesn't matter how the heck it's going to happen. Just get a result that feels right. This is so, so easy. It takes about five seconds.

Let's imagine you want to find a great new house to live in, even though the rental market's really tight in this part of town. You don't want to spend weeks searching, so forget that. You don't want to pay more than is fair, so forget that too. What would feel great is finding the perfect house easily, cheaply and out of the blue. By looking at the solutions that feel a bit tense and disappointing, you find the feeling you actually want to achieve. Note that feeling, and you've got the perfect direction for your magick.

Then come up with your question. You phrase this as though your wish was granted sometime in the past. It would be absolutely fine to use that example I gave earlier. 'How did I come to own this beautiful piano?' Asking that feels good. For the rental property, it might be, 'How did we find such a beautiful, low-cost house so easily?' Or even simpler, 'How could it be so easy to find the perfect house?'

It's really easy to stuff this part up by problem-solving, and trying to define exactly how the magick should work. Don't tell the magick how to work. Don't insist that the only way to get your piano is by winning the lottery. It *isn't* the only way, and it's probably the least likely.

I'll try not to repeat this too often, or you're going to find me boring, but, you know, just to make sure... Magick can find really, really inventive ways to get things to appear in your life. You do a ritual for a piano, and out of the blue, your neighbor decides to move to Montana and leaves her piano for you. Thank god you didn't waste your time telling magick that you needed *money* for the piano. You only needed the piano.

Pianos are not the smallest of objects, and you probably don't want one. I did, and I got one. But, when you're starting out, you might want to aim for something that's a bit closer to your current reality. When you first get into magick, it's tempting to go straight for those massive goals that have been obsessing you forever. Aim a bit lower. Don't aim so low that it feels pointless; no point in doing magick for a good lunch when you can just go out and buy a good lunch. But you could do magick to get somebody to be kinder to you, or to pay what they owe you, or to stop their dog from barking at night. Think of a small thing you *really* want to change; something that's possible, but that you have no direct control over.

You're not going to levitate or become famous by next week. Look for something you want that's out of reach, but within the realms of possibility if the magick were to give reality a twist. It has to be a real desire, or there'll be no emotion.

You might want to avoid money magick when you're setting out unless it's for a really small amount. Most people have pretty big hang-ups about money, and huge doubts about money magick ever working…and then they just cannot stop watching and waiting for the result. When you watch and wait, you get more watching and waiting. Avoid money for now. Don't worry. Money magick works, but find your feet with something else first.

Chapter 5: Emotional Crafting

You're now going to use an emotion-based method to create a sigil. It's so easy that you'll wonder if it's magickal at all, but I can promise you that it is.

At this point, you've got a goal, and you've created a magickal question in the past tense. In our example, the question is, 'How did I get this beautiful piano?' or something similar.

For you it could be:

'How did I learn to control my anger?'
'Why am I so at ease in social situations?'
'Why is my boss so kind to me these days?'
'How did my sales get so high this year?'

Or anything else you like. The magick can be aimed at changing you, your luck, the people around you, or manifesting something physical that you desire.

Now we come to the second part of sigilisation. This is where traditional Chaos Magick would have you create a scribbly doodle out of all the letters. If you've seen this all before, I know, it can be pretty boring. Bear with me for a few paragraphs, try not to yawn, and we'll get somewhere interesting.

Traditionally, this is how you turn a bundle of letters into a sigil. You write down your magickal statement (in our case, it's a question, but traditionally it's a statement such as, 'I am a wealthy person'). Ok, you write that down, and then you get rid of some letters. Sometimes you omit duplicate letters and vowels, sometimes you just put everything together.

Whatever method you use, you create a drawing out of the remaining letters. What you end up with looks like a sort of mashed up tree of letters. Something like this:

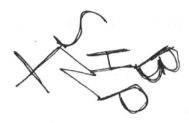

Often it's more intricate, as there are lots of letters. Then you redraw it, by scribbling about again, making it look less like letters.

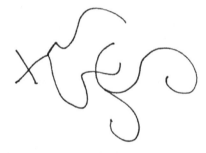

And then you might redraw it again, trying to make it look a bit like a magickal sigil.

Eventually, after more messing around with your doodle-scribble, it may look something like this:

Redrawing just means that you draw it again, taking out the bits you don't like, changing anything you want. There are no rules at all, so you never *ever* need to wonder if you're doing it right. The drawings don't matter. What matters is that you started with letters from your question and squiggled them into a sigil.

You keep drawing until you get to a point where the squiggle no longer reminds you of the letters you started with, or of your goal. That's that idea with traditional Chaos – *you must forget your goal.*

Can you imagine how difficult that it is?

'I really want to get a promotion, but now that I've done magick for the promotion, I'll just forget about it. Wait a minute... I forgot to apply for the job.'

A variation on the theme that we've encouraged is that you forget about the magick, but not the goal. It's ok to think about your goal. You think about it as though it's an inevitable pleasure, and that defuses the fear. But you forget about the magick.

In one of Damon Brand's books, he explains a sigilisation method that uses this method more directly. Rather than trying to forget the goal, you create a sigil that actually *represents* your goal, because you don't need to forget about it. This is the number one myth when it comes to traditional Chaos Magick. You will always be told that when you fire your sigil with a moment of magick, you must then forget about your goal. If you think about your goal at all, it short circuits occult reality, and your chosen desire cannot come to pass. I'm pleased to tell you that this is pure fiction.

You *can* think about your goal, so long as you don't sit around doubting the magick itself, and hoping that the magick's going to work. The goal is something you can dwell on, happily. But don't sit around thinking about your ritual.

Damon's method is a good one – creating an abstraction that *feels like your goal*, meaning you never have to put the goal out of your mind.

The process I like to use is similar but goes a bit further. Forget about converting letters into a doodle. You don't need the letters at all. Instead, you say your question out loud, while moving your pen around on a piece of paper. It's not exactly automatic writing, but it's a bit like that.

If your question is, 'How did I come to own such a beautiful piano?' you say that out loud while moving your pen around on a piece of paper.

Use any paper. Use a pencil if you prefer, or finger-paints. The artwork just happens by itself. Say the question out loud a few times; the most important thing is that you *feel the question* while your pen moves. Feel as though you have your result, that it came some time ago, and that you're looking back in bliss.

Without that feeling, you're just a noisy robot who's drawing something rubbish. Feel the question, and scribble away.

What you end up with may not look so elegant. It may look like this:

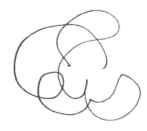

Or this:

Or this:

Great artistry is *not* required. Phew.

You can do a couple of things now. If you feel like it, declare that this is your sigil and use it in the next stage of the ritual. Or you can refine it. There's no need to think or feel anything as you refine; you just redraw the best bits, or the bits that you like.

You might take that last scribble and make it look like this:

And with one more refinement it could look like this:

And then you declare that *this* is your sigil. You don't have to say, 'This is my sigil,' out loud. You just decide that this is it and that the work is complete.

I like to put a circle around it because it makes it feel universal yet contained, as well as just looking a bit more magickal than a doodle.

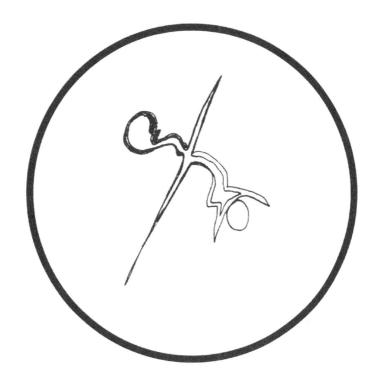

The sigil is a way of summing up your magickal intent in a visual form.

Feel the question. Say it out loud. Draw something. Refine it. You're ready for magick. In fact, you've already done some magick. Notice that you have performed emotional alchemy, and it was effortless. You had a problem (or a goal you desired) that you felt one way about, and then by asking yourself a question about your result in the past tense, the emotion changed. The act of creating the sigil means that the magick is already bubbling away.

Chapter 6: The Fire of Gnosis

Once you've created your sigil, the traditional approach is to fire it into the abyss of chaos, whatever that means. In practice, you look at the sigil when you are in a highly excited state or an alternate state of consciousness. This state is often called gnosis, and the most common method to achieve gnosis is sex, or (if we're honest) masturbation. You glance at the sigil during masturbation, right on that moment of orgasm. You 'drink in' the image into your mind at that moment of ecstasy, and then you throw the sigil away and forget about it.

There are other approaches to gnosis, such as slight suffocation, dancing, days of meditation, fasting, exhaustion and so on, but I've never found those appealing or effective. It sounds a bit much, and a bit too boring. You hear about people doing a five-hour dancing ritual to get into a state of exhaustion, just to make a bit of extra money, and I think, you know, you'd be better off if you just went out and did five hours of paid work. Sounds cynical, but magick is meant to make things easier overall. Suffocating yourself is too much hard work.

In traditional chaos, you might be advised to create several sigils so that you don't actually know which one you're firing. This is so you avoid thinking about your goal. That isn't required, and I think it's way better to make sigils only for things you actually want to change than it is to do lots of random and weak magick. Make a sigil like you mean it, and fire it up with passion.

You've got your sigil - time to fire it. Most people are sexually active to some degree, so I really can't argue with the orgasm method. It works so well that there's not much to argue with. Do that, and you get results. Or you can get as creative as you like. I once took a sigil with me on a very intense rollercoaster and made sure it was within my line of sight as I went through the trauma of that event. It worked.

For me, roller coasters definitely bring on an altered state of consciousness, because I'm terrified of them.

You can carry a sigil and wait for an appropriate real-world event that, by its nature, brings about altered consciousness. Say you almost have a car crash, a near miss that could have been fatal. You're enraged, heart racing, parked at the side of the road in wonder that you're alive. This is an altered state. You glance at the sigil. This works, because it's an altered state of consciousness quite unlike normal reality. The main drawback with this approach is that you need to wait around for such incidents, and you can go months without one.

Another method is just to leave the sigil lying around as though it's not that important. The image gradually seeps into your subconscious without any grand ceremony or moment of gnosis. You can even create a painting or some other artwork out of the sigil and hang it on your wall so that it's always there, being taken in, but never really looked at. This passive approach is fine for long-term workings. But I know most magicians are an impatient lot, so I think firing off a sigil with gnosis is better.

My opinion is that you should create the sigil and fire it within a day of its creation. Orgasm is the quickest and most tempting way. If you're not interested in the orgasm method and don't have a rollercoaster nearby, and if you've wisely chosen to avoid self-suffocation (because it really does lead to accidental death a lot of the time), what are the alternatives? Anything that puts you in an altered state of consciousness will work. Although having said that, I don't believe drugs work. Drugs are popular with some occultists, but I think they make you dozy, dim-witted, sleepy, distracted, hyped up or otherwise out of it, and although your consciousness *is* altered, I think too much of your brain is offline or over-wired for gnosis to be as good as it could be. If you really don't want to do the orgasm thing, chanting is a good way to get out of your mind fairly quickly.

When you become familiar with occult material, you begin to suspect that many of the words chanted in the really long rituals are there just to make you babble away in a non-language so that you lose track of reality a little. That's ok, but there are some chants that do have meaning, and also seem to alter consciousness when chanted for ten minutes or more.

Here are five you can choose from, or you can use them all at once.

EE-AH-OH-EH

EE-ADD MOZZ ZEER

AH-RAH-BEATER

LEH-VAH-NAH

AH-RAH-BAH-OO-AH-RAH-BAH

These are divine names, magick opening words and such like, from eclectic sources. Focus on the sounds, and the archetypal meaning will slip through into your reality and shift your consciousness. (Could you make up any sound and get the same effect? Maybe. Probably not. *Some words are better than others.*)

Chant these out loud for ten minutes, and you will start to feel something. Focus only on the sounds and your body (not on the magick, or hope, the day you've had, or anything else), and you will shift to a dreamy state of consciousness. While chanting, you look at the sigil, and it's done. It's not the most intense gnosis, but it works. Orgasm is quicker, more intense. But, chanting does work if you can stay focused on the sound of the chant rather than drifting off in thought.

Now let's take this up a level.

If you add *emotion* **to the moment of gnosis, the magick is far stronger.**

And what's magnificent to know is that *any emotion will do*. It doesn't have to be positive, pure or in any way related to your goal. Emotion, in this instance, is just like throwing fuel on the fire. It is raw power. You don't need to transmute the emotion; you just feel it. Got a load of pent-up anger or hatred? This is where you can use that anger up, take the fire out of it, and put that power into your magick.

Emotions are interesting; frequently a side effect of your current state of mind. You think thoughts, you exist in a particular moment, and emotions spring up to reflect that moment. As such, there are many psychological systems and philosophies that can help you get in touch with your emotions and the sensation in your body (which reflects the emotion), to know yourself. This can be useful, of course. However, for gnosis, rather than trying to know yourself through emotions, you can direct your emotions to make yourself what you choose to be. This is not about feeling positive and trying to assure yourself that you're happy, it's about accessing any raw emotion. Whether it is a dark and satisfying emotion, something light, deep or beautiful, it will energize the magick like nothing else.

If you want to know why, I think it's two things. Magick is all about carving out reality with emotion as a guide. Although magick uses imagery and outside help (from spirits), the shaping force is your emotional state. It is the essence of magick. I believe that emotion gives you direct access to belief. People try to shift their beliefs and pretend to believe something, but the truth is that our beliefs are formed not through habits of thought, but from repeated emotional responses. We come to believe the things we believe because of the way we have felt about them. Our thoughts are less relevant. When you hit the moment of gnosis, the energy of emotion is the energy of change, and it can scorch a new belief into your soul.

How do you make an emotion appear? One of the best ways is through memory. Recalling a memory that triggers an emotion is easier than just cooking up the feeling out of nowhere. Some people can just feel things, just like that, no effort involved. If that works, voila. It not, try memory.

When you start out a ritual, you know you don't yet have your result. That's your belief. You reframe your result as a question, set in the past tense, so it feels more like a reality. You've created a new belief – the belief that your result is a reality. You may not believe it yet, *but the belief exists as a sigil*.

You then absorb that image into your deepest self, using gnosis. When you add emotion, you marinade that sigil with the force of change. It becomes a belief on the deepest level. And reality changes to match it.

Earlier, I went on about affirmations, and how they don't work. No matter how often you tell yourself 'I am a confident person,' if you don't feel confident, it is unlikely to change your belief. When you perform magick, you are changed on the deepest level. Your emotion changes, the belief enters your soul, and from there flourishes and bursts out to affect you and your reality.

When you're doing the magick, you reach gnosis, and you feel something intensely. That's it.

Let's pretend we're still working on getting that piano. We've created a sigil, and we're about to fire it. What emotion should we choose? It really doesn't have to have anything to do with the piano, with magick, or anything in particular. The crucial thing is to find something you can feel easily.

If you're in the middle of a ghastly argument with your ex-lover this week, your emotions are doubtless on the surface. Use them. If you're enraged about something today, use that. If you've fallen in love, use that. If there's nothing close at hand, think of a potent memory. Work over that memory in your mind until you can feel the emotion of it. Use that.

Here's what you do. You've chosen your emotion, and you now turn your attention to reaching gnosis. You may choose to slam a hammer down on your thumb (it works, but I really, really don't recommend it), or you may go for something else inventive that switches you out of normal consciousness, or you may chant, or you may just choose orgasm. If you're canny, you'll know that orgasm really is the best way, and it's fun.

You do whatever it takes to get to gnosis. In this example, we'll assume it's orgasm. You head off toward orgasm, and when you know you're almost there you recall the emotion. Now, this can take a bit of practice. As orgasm approaches, your mind tends to fade away to nothing. But your feelings don't. It's easy to feel while you orgasm. The secret is to trigger the emotion just before orgasm. Too soon and it might get in the way of your lustful pleasure. Too late, and well… it's too late. But if you time it just right, you will probably feel that emotional energy flare up beautifully during the orgasm. And if the sigil is within your line of sight, the magick is done.

Think about a time when you made love to somebody that you love, truly and deeply. When you achieve orgasm, you can feel your emotion of love in a truly explosive way. This is a very different experience than less emotional sex or sex that's just for fun. When you really love, and when you feel that love in the moment of orgasm, it's a wonderful thing. Not everybody gets that. Some people focus only on the sensation. Others start to feel guilty as they get to orgasm. But if you're lucky, then you will know that orgasm can take the emotions you offer, and fill them with power. That's the secret of this advanced gnosis.

Use this process with your sigil. Feel an emotion, any emotion. Feel it just before you orgasm, and let the orgasm take that feeling. Look at the sigil. The orgasm and the emotion will then fade.

Let yourself return to normality in the slow, dreamy, lazy haze of sexual afterglow, just as you would anyway. Avoid looking at the sigil. I screw the thing up straight away and throw it aside. After the moment of gnosis, it's ok to see the image – the universe won't collapse if you do - but you really don't want to be pondering it now. Put it aside, because it is now within you. You can throw the sigil away. Burn it ceremoniously if you want, and scatter the ashes at the roots of an oak tree. Or do what I do - trash it with the mashed potatoes and onion scraps. It's garbage now.

Forget about the magick as best you can. You don't have to force it from your mind, but the magick is done, so move on.

If you have friends who are into magick, an interesting experiment is to fire each other's sigils. Your friend makes a sigil and does not tell you what result is being sought, and you fire it for them. They fire one for you in return. I'm not suggesting you do this in the same room at the same time (although some adventurous types do that!), but that there is an exchange. I don't think this is a necessary technique at all because chaos is so often personal, but it really works for some people. Worth trying once you've mastered the basic approach to firing a sigil.

And that's it for sigils. That's the core technique of chaos magick, remastered into something new. It works, and that's what matters, so find something you want to change and do the magick.

Chapter 7: Magickal Chaos Energy

Spend any time reading magick books you're going to see a picture that will soon bore you out of your mind. Yep, it's a sketch of the human body, showing chakras or energy points or some balls of light located in a column down the middle of the body. It's so ubiquitous as to be mind-numbing, but there is something worth knowing.

Flick through some modern manual of energy channeling or work with the traditional Middle Pillar Ritual, and it's all sort of the same, but all a bit different. Whatever tradition you subscribe to, there are balls of spinning energy at various points in the body connected by a column of light. Sometimes you circulate this light around the body too. And for what? Well, it helps build up magick energy. Bear with me. It gets better.

I'm not the first to say this, but it's a wee bit disturbing when you first find that some people say there are seven energy points right down the middle of the body, while others insist there are six. You're meant to breathe and circulate the energy of your breath through these points, so you want to know how many points there are. You don't want a debate about it. Nobody ever argues about how many lungs we have, or where the liver is situated. Why are these mystical energy nodes so difficult to pin down? Probably because they don't actually exist, objectively, in space and time. But they work. It doesn't matter how you do it, it works. There is something inherently magickal about breath and light and balls of energy. If you think I sound pretty ridiculous right now, you should know that many of the most serious occult works don't talk about much more than these balls of whizzy-dizzy energy. There's got to be something to it.

Now, if you've got some religious reason for believing there are seven, twelve or some other number of energy centers in the body, don't let me change your mind. But, if you've never heard about any of this, or just want to start over with something easy and workable, here we go.

After all that preamble, the description of the magick is going to be so short you'll think it's something you can skip. And it is. Energy work is not magick, but it's *magickal* and can be used in a handful of practical ways.

Step 1. The obvious bit.

Do the usual magick prep stuff – stand quietly where you (probably) won't be disturbed. There's no danger if you are disturbed; it's just easier to do this well if you don't have to empty the dishwasher part way through.

Step 2. The breathy bit.

Focus on your breath. The very words 'focus on your breath' make me think back to yoga and Pilates classes that I never enjoyed, but yeah, focus on your breath. But, instead of just noticing it going in and out, imagine that as you draw air in, it transforms into a glittery light. You're filling your lungs with light. Way more fun than Pilates. Do this for a minute or two, nice deep breaths, but not so deep that you hyperventilate. Some people consider this light to be absolutely real; an actual energy. For the sake of this magick, you can do the same.

Step 3. The fun bit.

Circulate the light! As you breathe in, that light from your lungs expands so much that it ascends to the crown of your head. You can picture a white laser beam, a foggy mist, or anything else you like, but keep it so that it could reasonably be called 'a column of white light.' You breathe out, and nothing happens. With the next inhale, the light again swells up from your lungs, all the way through the column of light that is there. It pours out of the top of your head and spills down your body. In some traditions the light arcs all around you, but think of this as liquid light. You're in a shower! The light comes out of your head and just spills all the way down to your feet. It might take a few breaths for you to imagine this light spillage to reach your feet.

Step 4. The dizzy-magick bit.

Suck it up! When the light reaches your feet, you take another breath, and the light rushes through your feet, forming another column of light. It meets your lungs, and with every breath, this continues. Quite a lot to imagine, isn't it? Light coming in, light rising up spilling down and rising up again. Just do your best. You will almost certainly start to feel a bit magickal around now. You may be building energy, or you may just be breathing too hard, but you will feel something.

Step 5. The bit with the lights.

I never liked chakras or glowing balls of light. In some traditions, you picture different colored spheres at different parts of the body. It's fun, but you feel a bit like a Christmas tree. I like to create tiny stars of light. Minute pinpricks of utter brashness. Rather than locating these in the heart chakra, the throat chakra and all that, I allow the stars to appear where they will - within limits. I allow something like seven or so tiny pinpricks of light to appear within the column of light, and they are brighter than the light that's already there. Sometimes they might form a perfect line, and other times they are scattered around the column of light. All I do is decide that I will allow these pinpoints of infinite existence to appear within me; it is very energizing. If you try it and find that nothing appears, just imagine some pinpricks of light where you want near the column of light. Job done.

Step 6. The bit where you stop.

Keep going, long enough to feel that you're building up a load of magickal energy, but not so long that you become exhausted or lose focus.

Is this any better than the Middle Pillar Ritual? I like it more, but you might not. The point is, if you don't, please make your own. It will work. Move light through the body, and through points or spheres, and you build your magickal energy. *Whoosh.*

You've made all this great magickal porridge. Now what? Seems a shame to just let it fizzle out. Here are some things you can try:

Put it into your sigils. Imagine the energy going into a sigil, before, during or after a ritual.

Put it into your magick. Get all worked up with energy and then do the ritual, and let that energy go into the magick. Try it, and you can see you don't need instructions. It happens.

Use it to heal. Lay your hands on something that hurts or is unwell, either on your body or somebody else's. Might help.

Be creative with this energy. My list ends here so you can think of your own ways to use magickal energy. There will be loads of times when you're reading this book, and you'll think, '*How can I add a bit of spice to that?*' This is how.

Chapter 8: Influence Magick

I have a close friend who believes that all magick is influence magick. You do a ritual for money, and it influences a hundred small decisions that make things go your way and bring you that money. I don't agree with him, but I think that influence plays a massive part in magick and that you can use direct influence to get what you want.

Seduction

Seduction magick is one of those subjects that's always made me squirrely. If you sway somebody's mind with magick, how's it any better than date rape? But then one lovely night I was seduced, by magick, and I can say with certainty that I was not drugged, doped, tricked, forced or lured into the seduction. It was a relief. An impossible situation was brought to an end, and something exquisite came out of it. I was taken to place I hadn't thought or dared to go. No complaints here. I think to some degree I knew that I was being seduced, in the same way you know when somebody is staggeringly, obviously beautiful, open, and flirtatious. So I suppose it almost felt like normal seduction.

The magick I'm about to give you only works about six times out of ten, and it only works if you've got some degree of courage. Six out of ten might even be generous. But, that's not too bad.

Only use it when you want it to work – don't test it out on people just to see if it works and then walk away. It works best when you seriously want it to work. Your genuine desire gives it some muscle.

In a nutshell, this is what you do. You make brief eye contact with your subject, and during that moment you look with real love in your heart. No magick words, no tickling auras, no sexy demons to raise the heat. Pure love, straight to the eyes. If that sounds way too easy, know that if you get it just slightly wrong, you're going to look like a creepy stalker.

You're at the party. The subject of your desire is standing nearby, so that eye contact is possible. You make normal eye contact a few times. Then you look away and conjure up a feeling of real love. Who do you love? Think about somebody you love, some great passion, and then look back at the subject and feel as though you are looking at the one you love. It doesn't have to be romantic love that you feel. Just love.

Keep it really short, without looking like you're too embarrassed to hold eye contact. Extended eye contact is great for flirting, but this kind of eye contact is magickal and will feel intrusive if it goes on too long.

If conjuring up love feels like too much, you can modify it, and do it like a method actor. What do you look like when you gaze at somebody you love? How do you feel when you look into the eyes of your beloved cat? The next time it happens, when you really adore somebody or something, get the feeling, remember it, store it up. Unless you're a hermit, it shouldn't take much time to find a way to practice this gaze. Get to grips with it, and then learn to bring the gaze on by itself. Practice on a flower or a door handle. Practice! This loving gaze doesn't just feel like you're looking at somebody you love, but like you're bestowing love. When you can conjure that up for a door handle, you're ready for action.

There are so many variations. You can breathe the feeling of love onto your hand, right before you shake hands with the subject. Or stand nearby with the subject off to your left, and feel your body heat extend to wrap up the subject. There are many more, and you can make up your own. They might work. The eye contact one really works.

Don't expect your magick to be so super-powerful that you can prop up the bar and wait to be seduced. This eye contact magick is good, but it only creates a feeling of attraction. It doesn't cause direct action unless you're lucky. Go make conversation and, if you want, do the eye contact magick one more time. Only do it once more though, and only when you're speaking and the subject is listening. That's when it sinks in and has an effect.

Object Influence

At one of the darkest times of my life, there was a crazy couple doing everything they could to get me in trouble. It's a familiar story, almost a cliché. You make friends with a couple. They get really attached, almost clingy, draining. Then, when you try to cool things down because the friendship is a bit too intense, they turn on you with utter spite. You go from being friends to getting threatened and harassed.

I was young, desperate to get away from these people, and I didn't have magick that could help me. I knew some magick, but not as much as I do now, and I didn't have any defense against this sort of attack. I sought the help of the local witches. No kidding. Through a friend of a friend, I managed to track down this couple who were known to practice witchcraft, and I begged for their help.

I didn't mention that I knew anything about magick and asked them to do the magick for me. But they told me to do the spell myself. It was so basic. Two black candles, no magick words, no gods, nothing. All I did was put two candles on the floor next to each other and light them. As the dark and stormy night raged on, I moved the candles apart ever so slightly. Not so fast that it would create resistance, but a gradual parting. By the time the candles burned out, in the early hours, they were on opposite sides of the room.

But the interesting bit is this. One candle was me. The other candle was the couple. I wasn't moving candles. I was moving us apart, breaking the bond.

I did not say 'one candle represented me.' It *was* me. That's what those lovely witches told me. You don't pretend the candle is you, you accept that it is. Use your imagination, and as the ritual plays itself out, your feelings change. When you light those candles, you feel the cloying togetherness. As they move apart, you feel a steely calm. When they're on either side of the room, you feel relief and freedom.

You accept that one thing is actually another thing or person, and then you do something to that thing. You let this change how you feel. This is a way to influence people. You can change minds and feelings, and get decisions to go your way. You can do this for just about anything, so long as you are able to accept that one thing is another thing for the duration of the ritual.

You don't use your imagination intensely. There's no need to visualize that the candle is you, you just suspend disbelief. Accept that it is. Do the magick. It might take practice to get this right, but any time you want to change a mind, this will work.

Doesn't have to be candles. To separate a couple, you could write their names on a piece of paper, and slowly tear the paper down the middle, to separate the names, then move those pieces apart.

You could take a delicate object, such as a glass, and accept that it *is* a relationship between two people. Shatter the glass, and the relationship shatters. Are you sure you want it to shatter? Might be better to craft a ball of clay, *know* that it is the relationship, and leave it out in the rain so it wastes away over a few weeks. Depends on how much spectacle you want.

It might take a bit of experimentation to find your style. You can do an elaborate ritual that goes all night to give a bit of substance to the occasion, make it feel like an event. Or keep it short, with one flash of focus and action. Something will work for you.

Gesture Magick

I never liked meditation until I heard about walking meditation. You walk around, and just look at stuff without thinking about it or judging it or drifting off into fantasy. I liked this idea because that was how I went for a walk anyway. No thought, no labels or names – just looking at stuff as I walked around. I can meditate!

But then I used my walks as self-influence magick, with something that I rather embarrassingly called The Success Walk. I decided that one thing meant another. Each time I went on a specific walk, that was an increase in my business success. The walk didn't represent success. It was success.

You make one action be something else. It can even be as abstract as success. This is slow burning magick that works on you better than it works on other people.

It worked for me, and it might work for you. If it doesn't, be glad of the exercise.

It also doesn't have to be a walk. You can use a hand gesture, a dance. If that gesture becomes a quality or experience you desire, then enacting that gesture increases that quality or experience.

I know this sounds crazy. 'Do a Happy Dance and you'll get happy!' No, I doubt it. But there is some substance here. I leave it to you to work out what's worth doing.

Document Magick

Say you want to change somebody's mind. You draw a simple sigil that represents the change. As you scribble it down, you think about how you feel now, and how you will feel when you have changed the other person's mind.

Your boss doesn't seem convinced by your request for a promotion. You draw a squiggly sigil while your emotions go from annoyance and frustration to relief and happiness that your boss has changed her mind.

Get that sigil in front of your boss. Methods include:

1. Leaving the sigil on a scrap of paper on the boss's desk. Your boss will look at it and then throw it away. But it's been looked at.

2. Using Photoshop or other image editing software, you add the sigil to a logo, photo or another image. You make the sigil so tiny or faint that it can't be seen – but it's there. This has to be an image that you can send to your boss without raising suspicion.

3. Drawing the sigil with a light pencil on a paper document, then erasing it. A trace of the sigil will remain, and that is enough.

The bit you have to get right is the feeling – the feeling you have when you draw the sigil. Get that right, and it works. There's another method that requires a good imagination. You imagine that you are the other person. Take your time. Take on the expressions and body language of your boss. Feel the negative feelings your boss has about your request. Start drawing your sigil. Then change your mind. Imagine being your boss and feeling good about hiring you. Now get that sigil in front of your boss.

I used the example of your boss, but you might not have a boss. You can use this on anybody, but it's best if you know the person. You can try this with strangers, but it's not quite as effective.

This chapter needs to mention thoughtforms because thoughtforms have an influence on people. They do more than influence, though, so they get half a chapter all to themselves. Coming right up.

Chapter 9: Thoughtforms and The Other People

Before we ask for the help of spirits (which works whether you believe in them or not), let me show you two aspects of magick that made me cringe with embarrassment when I first tried them. They work so easily that they can't be ignored.

When I was in my teens, me and my friends found a mail-order publisher of occult books, and we worshipped it. So much potential! The adverts for those books were wild and over the top, and we'd save up our pocket money and send off for the books. We'd wait a week or so, and the books would arrive looking kind of cheap and creepy, but they also looked like they might actually contain some real magick. We'd order books, one after the other, and wait impatiently, hoping there'd be something we could use. We were often disappointed because the magick turned out to be too serious or too vague or, worst of all, too silly.

There was one book about thoughtforms; it was left in my care, and I lost it decades ago, and can't even remember the name of the author. But, the essence of that book was that you made up some imaginary friends, and so long as you talked to them as though they were real, they could do magick for you. I was enraged. That seemed so dumb I wanted to tear the book up. That may be what actually happened, because I have a pretty all-encompassing room full of occult material, and that book is nowhere to be found. Never mind.

I rejected the ideas wholly and moved on to a wicca ritual with an onion. It didn't work. But at least I wasn't playing with imaginary friends.

A couple of years later, working with Chaos Magick, I chose to develop a few servitors. To create a servitor, you invent a spirit that is bound to you, and it does magick for you when asked. You treat the servitor as though it's real. You birth it with some sort of occult energy and ceremony. Cool. But here's an alternative: thoughtforms. And yes, although it sounds daft, they are a bit like imaginary friends that you talk to so often that they become real. I wouldn't put you through this if it didn't work, so bear with me.

Thoughtforms work most reliably when they are used on your own flaws and shortcoming (or skills and strengths), and when they're used to influence the feelings and thoughts of others.

A thoughtform does not need a ritual, sigil, or physical place to reside, or anything else that goes into crafting a servitor. It only needs repetition. If you invent a creature and imagine that it is there often enough, it's there. There are many hardcore occultists who laugh their pants off at this. Unless you're commanding demons, you're just not tough enough! The funny thing is, it takes great bravery to pretend that there's something there when there isn't. This is the magick of real courage because you risk feeling like an idiot; when you first get into this, you might wonder whether you've lost your grip on sanity. When you actually sense or see the thoughtform, it can be just as staggering as a full demonic evocation. That's why I don't call this silly anymore. If you have the knack for it, this is heady magick.

I've rambled on for a bit because the actual technique is only a couple of sentences long: you pretend something is real, and imagine it's there. Eventually, it is there, and then it can do stuff for you.

You might imagine a glowing ball of light, or a horned alien, or something angelic, or a magickal cat, or a wispy mist. You might give it a name. You might give it a face, a personality, a particular set of powers. There are no rules. You just keep your attention on it, with these thoughts in mind. One day, you sense that it has consciousness, and off you go. You just speak to it and tell it what you want to happen.

I used to be nervous around girls in my early teens, so I made a thoughtform that would make me relax when I was near them. I imagined a blue-skinned man, walking by my side, on the left. I knew that he made me calm. I kept it simple. He didn't make me interesting, or good at flirting – just calm.

That was all I wanted. I'd imagine him there any time it occurred to me, which was hundreds of times a day. If I turned my head to the left and looked for him, I'd see him. All in my imagination... until it wasn't. Until I could think of him and catch a glimpse of him, more alive than imagination could ever make him. And then I asked him to walk with me, make me calm. And he did.

Make something up, pay attention to it, and then ask it to do what you want.

If your thoughtform ever feels a bit too alive or rebellious, or like it's not doing what you want, you can imagine it being killed, torn apart, dissolved, or melted. Your imagination rules, so you win these battles.

It sounds easy, and it is, but it does take a fair bit of effort to keep believing in something you know isn't real. It can take weeks before you ever get to ask for magick, and your head can get pretty cluttered. Build fifteen thoughtforms, and you find they pop up when you're trying to do other magick. It's distracting, so keep it under control.

Another form of magick that enraged me was anything involving an effigy or doll. The idea of making effigies in wax, clay or anything else was childish, and because I'd seen it in horror, movies it felt more like fantasy than reality. Until I tried it.

You create an effigy out of anything you like and act as though it's the person you want to affect. You don't pretend it's *like* the person or *connected* to the person, you act as though it *is* the person. You talk to it. You feel toward it, the way you do toward the person. You have the same mannerisms when you're around it. This might take a few minutes or a few days, but when the effigy starts to feel real, you do the magick – and that happens like this. You build your feelings toward the effigy (which are identical to the feelings you have for the actual person), and then as you stroke, mangle or otherwise affect the clay figure, you change your feelings. If you want to shut the mouth of the doll, you literally shut it, and feel enormous satisfaction that the person's mouth is shut.

Whether you sew, squash or just squeeze the lip together, this works. Use your imagination, and you can have an enormous effect on people with this magick. Even if it seems silly. You can do obvious harm to your effigies, but you can also bind them up, freeze them, wrap them up together, or put ideas (on little scrolls of paper) right into their heads. Lots of places you can go.

Don't let yourself end up with a cupboard full of effigies. When your magick has worked, look at the effigy as a stranger would. It's not the person you believe it to be; it's clay and cloth and wire and feathers. Look at it like a scientist would. Take it apart with the same lack of feeling that you would have taking apart a broken toy, and then throw it away.

There's another way to get this to work, which is to create a single effigy that you think of as a powerful magickal being. Take at least a month to build your little person, and know that as you do so, it is coming to life. Yes, this should feel a bit creepy; this magick gives me the shivers. I don't know why making a tiny clay person should feel like you're giving birth to a real lifeform, but this happens. You build your magickal person slowly, adding new bits. Keep it hidden away, at the back of a drawer, or behind a box. Make it feel like something naughty or secret. Visit it each day and add something new – maybe just another blob of clay, or a bit of gravel for texture. Feed it magickal energy. When it feels like it's almost alive, give it eyes. Even if you just stick a couple of old buttons on the face, those eyes will look lively. When it feels like it might have consciousness, you can do some magick.

Do not ask the effigy to do anything, just give it a sense of life and then tell it a story. Tell it your problem, and how you want to feel. Don't tell it how to solve your problem, just tell it the problem and how you want to feel when this is all over. It will do the work.

Remember when you used to tell your Grandma a story about how you were short of pocket money, and how much you'd like to buy that new *Star Wars* toy, and Grandma would magickally solve the problem for you? She wouldn't hand you the cash there and then, but she'd make sure you got the cash. The same is true of your little effigy. Tell it a story, and it will listen and work to solve your problem.

Who the hell is doing the magick here? Is it your will, your imagination, another lifeform, or does the effigy call on other spirits? This isn't a theory book, so we won't go into that, but I will say that even though this sounds like the most ludicrous part of the book, it's really worth working with. But you need an active imagination. If you're the sort of person that walks past a graveyard and starts imagining all sort of strange feelings, or if you go into a house and sense things that aren't obviously there, this is going to work beautifully. If you can be playful and childlike and commit to this magick, no matter how daft it seems, it will shock you. It may also fail utterly… but, that's magick. Most of the time, it tends to work. Sometimes it doesn't, but that's how you find the magick you want to work with for the rest of your life.

If you like your effigy, keep it hidden, and you can use it indefinitely. If you don't like it, pull it apart and drop it in a bucket of water. This can be unpleasant – I can't lie about that. You just have to get it done, pour the remains away and tell yourself that it was just a toy and that it's gone.

No book on Chaos Magick would be complete without a chapter on Servitors. OK, sorry, this book is incomplete. Damon Brand wrote *Magickal Servitors*, and I couldn't add anything to that. I gave you a chapter on thoughtforms and The Other People instead. Most Chaos Magick books don't give you that, so can we call it even? Thanks. (And there's a bit later on that shows you how to turn a thoughtform into a ceremonial spirit, so that's cool.)

Chapter 10: Upside Down Sex Magick

Chaos Magick can be at its most exciting when it takes an accepted faith and turns it upside down.

You've heard about the belief that whatever you hold in your mind becomes real. No, it doesn't – it just lingers there like a bad habit. Things become real when you *magick them*. Or when you destroy them; what you destroy with great imagination can become real.

Billions of hours have been wasted on the idea that what you visualize and hold in your mind becomes real. Goal-setting is an entire industry, with books, apps, camps, and cults. Acquiring your desire through the law of attraction is a religion. So, let's be Chaos Magicians and say *no thanks, we'll try the opposite*; we'll eradicate a goal and see what happens.

We'll take a goal, place it on a pyre and destroy it. And we'll do this will sex magick.

Sex magick! It works like this. Hold your desire in your mind at the moment of orgasm, imbue it with love and passion, and hey presto, you get your magickal reality. That's the normal way of things. So let's be Chaos Magicians and say, *no thanks, we'll try the opposite*. We'll use sex magick as a furnace where we burn our goals.

When you destroy a goal, the lack of attachment can make it easier to get something. Sex magick gives you a fiery energy. That's enough theory – let's burn stuff.

Find something precious and burn it. Think of a goal that evades, eludes, deceives or depresses you. A precious goal that you've been picking at and bothering with for years. You've waited for just the right ritual, the perfect angel, the best spell. Stop waiting. Take that goal and annihilate it with orgasm.

Summarize your goal as word, sound or image. Summon up all your feelings about the goal, and put them into a word, sound or image.

Sometime later, have sex. Good sex is better than average sex. That's not a tautology. I mean, good sex will give you better results than average sex.

When you reach orgasm, picture your goal-summary – imagine the sound, or the word. Let your goal be taken and destroyed by the fire of your climax.

Easy enough. What if you still feel your desire for the goal? Have you noticed that your goal doesn't feel as pushy, or as alive? It's not as interested in being real. It feels damaged.

Summarize the goal again; use the same summary or something new. Whatever feelings of desire you have left, pour them into this image, sound or word. There might not be as much to pour.

Your goal will vanish.

The worst that can happen is that you've freed yourself of an unattainable goal.

The best that can happen is that when you've moved on, your goal can finally make its way past the barriers of your fear and hope, and make itself real.

Short chapter, huh? Did you pick up the secret messages? I'm not going to spell it all out for you. But you get the idea, I know you do.

Be subversive.

But only when it works.

Chapter 11: Contacting Spirits

The foundation of most magick is any process that helps you get the paranormal assistance of a spirit. Spirits of all kinds can be asked, commanded and compelled to help you out. A lot of the time they do help, and if you are canny enough to ask for the right things in the right way, you can do very well with this magick.

By 'the right things,' I mean things that are *plausible but unlikely without magick*. You don't contact a spirit and ask for help with things that are probably going to happen without your magickal intervention. You also don't ask for the ability to fly or for instant, everlasting wealth and good luck. Reach for something that's just a little out of reach, and choose the right spirit for the job.

Ask a spirit to heal your heart, and you may find peace – but not if it's a spirit of destruction. Ask a spirit to banish your noisy neighbor, and you might get a result – but not if it's a spirit of love. Choose your spirits like you actually believe in them, whether or not you do.

By 'the right way' I don't mean you have to get your magick perfectly right; choose the right magick, do it well with full commitment, and let the magick do its merry business while you do yours.

When you get help from a spirit, your magick goes to a whole new place. You're no longer relying on your energy, your ideas or thoughts, or your wisdom – you get help. Spirits are good at getting things done, so asking them makes for good magick. They do the heavy lifting, the tedious and the unlikely, to get you what you want.

Angels and demons are the most obvious way to get into spirit contact, but there are many other types of spirits listed in occult literature – from genii to Olympic spirits. When working with Chaos Magick, you can work with the lot of them, finding the spirit that's just right for your current need.

You don't need to believe in the spirits, but you need to perform the rituals as though the spirits are real. Whatever your belief, it's your role to act out the magick. You might get a sense of the spirit's presence, you might go all shivery and goosebumpy, you might hear noises and whispers, or you might just feel a bit empty and weird afterward, as though you've wasted your time. That's ok. Keep doing magick; it feels less weird as you go, it starts working, and then you don't mind how daft you would look if somebody walked in on you while you were calling out to the angels.

Non-believers have done angel magick and have obtained what they asked for. It works because the angels respond when the magick is done sincerely. And by sincerely, I mean with feeling. Get the emotions right, and the magick all just slides into place. The magick just tends to work. (Some people believe it works because of quantum this-that-the-other and morphic fields, but we're leaving the theory out of this. I accept that the angels are real. You don't have to. It works anyway. Magick just does.)

To get help from a spirit, most occult systems suggest something along these lines:

Cleanse or confess and banish evil from the place where you work.

In lots of traditions, this is the main part of the magick. Snore. You fast, wash, and keep saying sorry until you feel you might be worthy, and you spend hours sending spirits away to make sure you don't get hurt by psychic troublemakers. Good news! Modern magick has made this bit super-fast. You don't even need to have a shower. A bit of mental prep can help, but it can be really simple.

Take on magickal authority.

This can be done by asking for God's permission, or by some other trick. Saying divine names and getting in the right state of mind is often enough to make a spirit take you seriously.

Get the spirit's attention.

Say some magick words, or do some magickal actions, to get the spirit to listen. You can use the spirit's sigil to make contact happen faster and more easily.

Tell the spirit what you want.

Talk clearly and say what you want. Power this up with emotional transmutation, meaning you tell the spirit what you want with your feelings.

Make an offering.

You can offer up some sort of payment at this point. This might be an offering – booze, flowery smoke (incense!), or a bit of food. You can also make a sacrifice or promise. "I'll give up smoking if you get me the money I ask for." *That* kind of sacrifice. No hurting of rabbits is required! Give up an addiction, or a pleasure. Some spirits love that because it actually costs you and shows that you mean what you say. You can also promise to spread the word about their good deeds; demons in particular love popularity. But, if you get to the essence of what I'm pushing in this book, you can keep the offering dead simple. Offer up gratitude, enjoyment, or pleasure with the results. Read any book by The Gallery of Magick and you'll see that this is all that's offered up, and it works. You can offer more if you want, but most of the time your feelings will be the key that unlocks the magick. You also offer to do your part of the work. The spirits handle the supernatural, but if you want things to happen you have to do ordinary things as well. If you want a promotion, you'd better work harder!

Get back to normal.

Let the spirit go off and do its stuff. The magick's working on some other plane now, so you get on with real life and let the spirit do the paranormal reality-mangling for you.

You do this by forgetting about the magick, and by having a busy and productive life.

And that works. With those instructions, some intelligence and quite a bit of creativity, I bet you could go out and get some sort of magickal result from some spirits. You'd need to do some research to find out a bit about the spirits first, but that's not too hard. It can be done. But, rather than talk about all the theories and ideas, I'll just get straight into an example that you can use: Olympic Chaos Magick.

Chapter 12: Olympic Chaos Magick

This chapter is a book within a book – a complete system of magick for contacting the Olympian spirits (which are usually thought of as angels). You can use this magick just as it's written, but in the next chapter, I'll show you how this magick was constructed from an ancient system. We cut out the bits we didn't need, to make something innovative and effective. Once you've seen how it's done, you can make up your own rituals. You don't have to, but if ever you really want to work with a particular spirit or entity, this will give you the indispensable tools you need for creating your own magick.

You might not know it now, but one day I bet you'll be digging your way through some old magick manual and you'll find a spirit that appeals to you. How to get its help? God knows how; there are no instructions, anywhere in the world. What to do? Using the ideas in the next chapter, you'll be able to contact that spirit.

But, let's leave that for the next chapter and get on with this chapter, which is the actual magick.

The spirits you'll be working with are Arathron, Bethor, Pahel, Och, Hagith, Ophiel, and Phul. They are known as the Olympic spirits. Here's how to say the names. (The *ah* sound is used a lot, so what does it sound like? *Ah* sounds like the *ah* you say when you sit down after a big day, or the sound you make when the doctor flattens your tongue to look at your tonsils. *Ahhhh*. Or, if you want to get a bit more technical, it sounds like the *ah* in father. F*aaahhhhh*ther.)

ARATHRON is pronounced
AH-RAH-THRON

BETHOR is pronounced
BETH-ORR

PHALEG is pronounced
FAH-LEG

OCH is pronounced
OWE-CH

HAGITH is pronounced
AH-GITH

OPHIEL is pronounced
OH-FEE-ELL

PHUL is pronounced
FOOL

When I say the name Phul, I picture the letters P-H-U-L, even though I pronounce it 'fool,' because the word 'fool' has a meaning that doesn't fit with my magickal aims. A small point, but there's merit in ironing out anything that makes the magick feel wrong to you.

The CH in OWE-CH is the CH you get in German ACHtung or Scottish LoCH. It sounds a bit like you're clearing your throat. You say the word OWE followed by this throat-clearing sound. If that sounds too difficult, just say OAK, which is near enough. (Any trouble with pronunciation? Just have a look at **www.galleryofmagick.com** and find the *Pronunciation and Spelling FAQ* page.

For GITH use the G sound you'd find in *give*, rather than the J sound in *jive*. And, before you think it's a misprint, that H in HAGITH is silent. AH-GITH.

You should know that these names could also be written and pronounced as Aratron, Bethor, Phaleki, Ock, Hageeth, Offiel and Full. These work as well. Magick just tends to work. We've picked our names and pronunciation, so now we work with the spirits like this:

Step 1. Choose a time, a place and a spirit.

Go to the place where you do magick and choose a single Olympic spirit that is best suited to your task. The place can be outside, inside, in a café (if you don't mind looking like a crazy person) or in front of the TV, so long as the TV is off. No temple or altar needed.

The best time of day is within the first hour after sunrise, but if you can't manage that, any time is ok, day or night. Work alone and make sure nobody's going to burst in on you. If you're in the café, sit where you won't be disturbed and ignore everybody.

Here's a menu of spirit powers to get you started and make your choice, along with each spirit's sigil:

ARATHRON

Arathron is associated with the powers of Saturn, and can:

Stop something in motion, whether it be a person, project or idea.

Destroy the wealth of an enemy.

Discover hidden sources of money.

End a project (yours or somebody else's).

Bind a person.

THE SIGIL OF ARATHRON

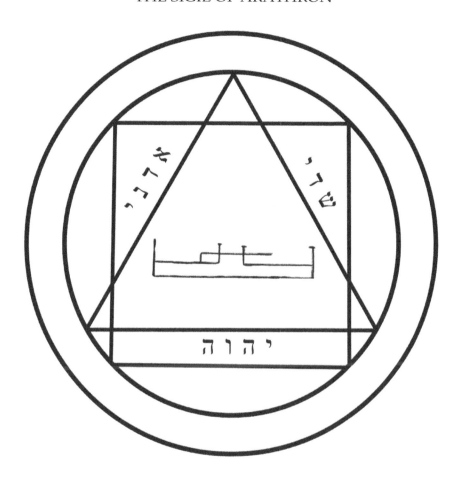

69

BETHOR

Bethor is associated with the powers of Jupiter, and can:

Give you great dignity.

Attract money from afar.

Make you appear valuable to those you encounter.

Increase luck when in conflict.

Increase your authority over others.

Aid in healing the self.

THE SIGIL OF BETHOR

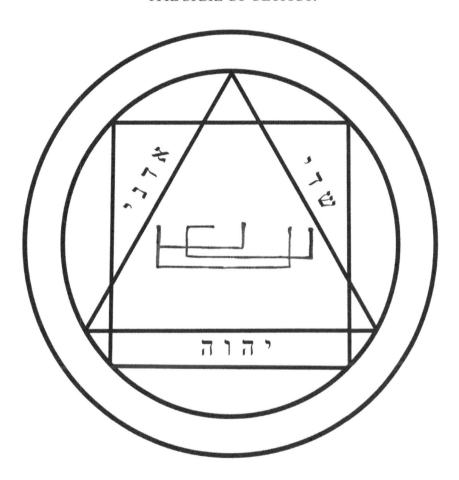

PHALEG

Phaleg is associated with the powers of Mars, and can:

Fight disease with vigor.

Strike fear into an enemy.

Defeat the efforts of an enemy.

Help you respond to attacks with cunning.

Attract others through calm authority.

Weaken the competition.

THE SIGIL OF PHALEG

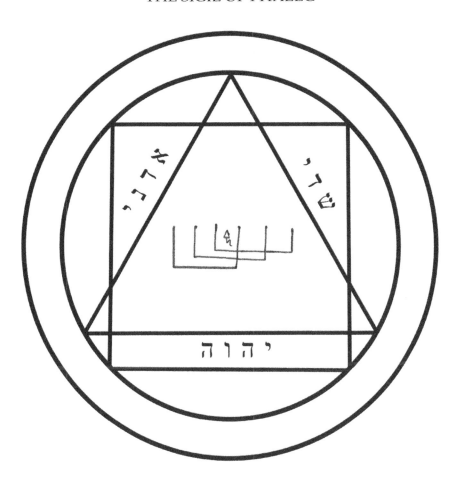

OCH

Och is associated with the powers of the Sun, and can:

Help you discover your true desires.

Inspire creative work.

Find new ideas related to business.

Bring the warmth of gentle healing.

Improve your reputation.

Enable you to work in peace.

THE SIGIL OF OCH

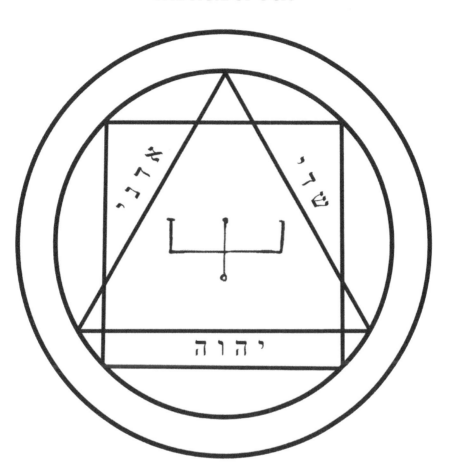

HAGITH

Hagith is associated with the powers of Venus, and can:

Improve sexual expression.

Change the mind of one you care about.

Attract those who can help you.

Attract love.

Attract friendship.

Cause lovers to part.

THE SIGIL OF HAGITH

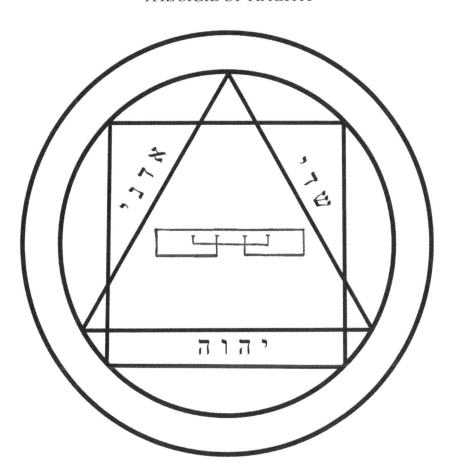

77

OPHIEL

Ophiel is associated with the powers of Mercury, and can:

Improve artistic expression.

Improve trade.

Ease mental suffering.

Enable good communication.

Spread the word.

Help you speak clearly.

THE SIGIL OF OPHIEL

PHUL

Phul is associated with the powers of the Moon, and can:

Enhance magick.

Improve intuition.

Slow the passage of time.

Cause another to dream about you.

Ease anxiety and fear.

Create sexual attraction.

THE SIGIL OF PHUL

You have to make a choice – which spirit and which power – and that compels you to use your intuition. Intuition means working with the intangible, so it's always a good warm-up for magick.

The power to 'end a project'... does that mean you end a project peacefully, like finishing the decorating on a Sunday afternoon, or does it mean that you bring an end to a project no matter what? This is Saturn we're talking about, which can be a heavy, destructive planet, so make your own guess!

When I say 'aid in healing the self,' does this mean you can heal a physical illness you have, or does it mean you heal your inner self? It can mean whatever you want it to mean. When I wrote this down, I meant that it was used for self-healing. But, this grimoire has been used for a fair while, and I know that others have used it in other ways, so you can usually be flexible in your interpretation of the meaning. It's Chaos Magick, not ceremonial ritual.

This is the way of grimoires. Things are left a bit loose, to give you room to use your intuition. Even though I was one of the people who created this system, I still have to look at this list of powers and have a think-and-feel about which would work best. I know loads more about Saturn, and I've read a lot about Arathron, but looking at this list and using your intuition – that is a time-tested way of doing magick.

Step 2. Confess your sins (Not really).

If confessing your sins to God works for you, go ahead. If not, this step can be skipped; but, why not be brave and take a moment to account for darkness and regret? I think of this as a little space in time where you can release pain, regret, and guilt. You're not confessing and saying sorry to God, but handing your troubles over to the Universe and saying, 'I'm done with all that now. Can you make me innocent all over again, so that I can go play? Thanks.' And then you do magick.

This is Chaos Magick so how you go about this is up to you, but my method is to think about my problems – my guilt, the things I feel bad about right now, today, and anything else that's still bugging me from years ago. I put my magickal goals aside and spend a minute or two feeling like crap about everything. Then I think about how stupidly tiny I am when I think about this street (because there are lots of people suffering here – I can just look out the window and see that on their face), and then I think about how small I am compared to this city, and then this country, and then this planet. And then, I think about the billions of stars and all of space and time, and I take that crappy feeling and just say, 'Thank you Universe for taking my troubles,' and I sort of act as though I'm handing over my heart – I physically move my hands forward – and it's done.

Instead of 'Universe,' you can say God, EE-AH-OH-EH or any other Divine name that occurs to you. If you're not religious, you still have to get that feeling of the size of the Universe. Hand your feelings over to that, and you're purified. (Some people confess to a tree or teddy bear, or some other thing they feel safe with. It's your life, so use a teddy bear if that appeals, but I think you get a bit more relief from the Universe.)

You're not going to absolve yourself completely of sin and regret, so don't expect this to make you pure and innocent for more than a jiffy. But for the sake of the ritual you're about to do, take a bit of time to let go of your troubles and pain and regret.

Step 3. Find Your Power.

This is all about authority, not energy. You can use the Magickal Chaos Energy before, during or after this ritual, but the power I'm talking about is the power to command. Angels, demons and the rest – they might like good manners, oh yeah – but they respond best when you speak to them as though you have the right to speak to them. If you plead with them, they're going to wonder why you think you have the right even to ask. But, have a feeling of authority, and you can get a response. You have the power and authority to tell them what you want. It can feel uncomfy ordering an angel around because you don't know what might happen next time you cross the road, but you can trust me when I say that you'll do better magick if you take on some authority. The moment you say, 'By the power of EE-AH-OH-EH,' the spirits sit up and pay attention. It doesn't matter that you didn't actually check with God to see if this was ok. You're saying that it's OK by God because you have free will, and that is authority enough.

There are loads of variations, but for this ritual, this is what we settled on:

"In the name of ADD-OH-NIGH, SHAH-DYE, and EH-AH-YEAH, I call on _____."

Have a look at the spirit's sigil. Let your eyes rest on the lines in the middle of the triangle because that's the important bit.

The call of authority is so short and breezy that it doesn't have much power unless you say it like you mean it, and act as though God (or the Universe or whatever else you like) granted you this power, and you're saying it proudly. Make the magick words vibrate so you can feel the word in your chest. If you're performing this ritual while sitting in the café you're doing this all in your head, so keep your mouth shut! Just imagine that it's really growly and makes your chest tingle.

Step 4. Call out to an Olympic spirit.

You called the name of the spirit when you did the authority bit, but there's nothing like repetition. Say the spirit's name while looking at the sigil; three times is enough. You can say is 333 times if you like, and then sit in peace until you feel the spirit's presence. That takes too long for me, so I say the name three times and believe the spirit's there. They find that difficult to ignore. It's like when you talk to somebody who's three rooms away, and they can't really hear you, but because you say their name they come right across the house to hear what you have to say. It's the same with spirits; say their name a few times, and they listen. Say it the same as you said the divine power bit, with the word so deep and powerful that you actually feel it in your chest. You might feel daft, or you might feel something change as the spirit becomes present – cold, warmth, pressure in the air. It doesn't matter if you don't see the spirit or if you don't feel anything magickal. Do what's written and then whatever happens, or doesn't happen, get to the point by taking the next step.

Step 5. Tell it what you want.

Keep your eyes on the sigil, without staring; just keeping it in sight and tell the spirit what you want. Just say it in plain, short, simple English (or whatever language you speak). Don't mime or use metaphors. Be clear; start with the spirit's name. Remember to tell it what you want with emotions. Tell a story. Start with the problem, and feel the problem. End with the solution and how that feels.

'Hagith, I do not know anybody who can help me develop my business. Hagith, I ask that you attract to me those who can help my business to flourish.'

Start every sentence with the spirit's name to make it clear you are addressing the spirit. When you say the first sentence, feel the problem. *I've got no friends to help...* Feel it! As you say the second sentence, imagine that Hagith *has* helped you find the friends that will help with your business. That's going to make you feel something. Feel it! It's OK to smile at this point.

Two sentences are enough. If you start going on about who's to blame and how this came about and different ways it can be solved, you're not going to get through. Make it short; pretend you're using Twitter. You've got one chance to make your point, so make it and feel it. Feel the change that you want to happen, and don't look forward to it, or you seal that feeling of hope into your future, which means that months from now you'll still be hoping. Feel it like it's already happened. Yeah, this takes some imagination, but that's what you need for magick. Your emotions don't have to be ultra-real and mega-powerful. The whiff of an emotion is enough fuel for the fire.

Step 6. Offering Up

Some say you don't need to offer up a thing, and most of The Gallery books agree with that. Sometimes, however, to get a spirit to pay attention to the physical world, it can be a lovely thing to offer up something physical. Right? You might want to give the spirit some cake or beer. How do you give cake to something that isn't there? You might build an altar, put a couple of candles there with the cake, and then throw it in the bin a day later assuming the spirit's had its fill. If this lights your fire, go for it. I avoid this style when I can, because I don't like to leave cake around the house – I may be tempted to eat it. Or it may go moldy. Or attract rats. However, some people just don't feel right about doing this sort of stuff without giving the spirits something to munch on. If you want to, go ahead. In Chaos Magick you are meant to be inventive, which means that if you want to know the rules for this, there aren't any. Make up your own. You can eat the cake, and pretend that the act of eating is your offering. Or leave it on a plate and assume the angel will descend for a bite at some point, or even throw it in a fire. Make something up.

What I prefer is to make a sacrifice or a promise of some kind. If I'm working with demons, this might be more of a bargain. "Give me this and I'll tell ten people that your magick works." For angelic beings, or spirits such as the Olympic spirits, I'll make a promise about a habit, thought or mood I want to change. Doesn't have to be life-changing, but still a change. Which makes it a win-win. If you're a smoker, don't offer to give up smoking just to get a date, or $100. Too difficult and you won't stick to it. Offer up something else. This week I am really sodding angry at bad drivers, so I'm going to give that up. I say to the spirit, 'Hagith, I sacrifice my anger at bad drivers.' Does it need more detail? No. I know what I mean, so Hagith knows what I mean. Keep it dead simple, and then stick to your side of the bargain. That driver pushes into your lane, you better be smiling. Why would Hagith care about this sacrifice? I sure as hell don't know, but this act of sacrifice is something that just about every spirit responds to.

Then there's good old gratitude. It sounds lame and makes you feel like you should be down at the crystal shop buying incense and rainbow bandanas, but gratitude seals the deal. You can offer it in advance by feeling grateful for the spirit's help. Nothing's happened yet, so you pretend. You can just feel it, or you can say, straight out, 'Take my gratitude for life, and for the result you bring me.' And, if you ever want to work with the spirit again, feel gratitude, *big* gratitude, when you get your result. That should be the case even when you offer up something else. If you want to keep it simple, gratitude is the only offering you need.

Step 7. Get normal.

Talking to spirits doesn't feel altogether normal. Even when you've been doing this for a handful of decades, the moments of magick can feel a bit out there, a bit strange. When it's done, you must get back to normal life.

At this point, tradition insists that you issue a license to depart, telling the spirit that it may go and do what you've already asked it to do. If you want, you can make a long speech about thanking the spirit for coming in peace, and letting it go in peace. A quick 'Thank you, Hagith,' will do the job nicely.

You then stand up (if you were sitting down) and splash cold water on your face, or open the window, or jog around the room. Something to feel normal. Well, not quite normal, but back in the real world. If you don't, the magick can be tainted by your thoughts and feelings, so you need to snap out of the magick and back to reality.

Afterward, tackle your problem as though magick doesn't exist. If you're trying to find inspiration for a song you want to write, sit at the piano and make music. Some spirits don't give a toss about the effort you put in, but most do, so get on with your life as though you can solve the problem without magick, and then let magick give you a surprise when it does work. If you sit there waiting for the jack-in-a-box to open, it will stay resolutely shut. Forget about the magick and let yourself be surprised.

Some magick you perform once, some eleven times, some thirty-three times. How many times do you want to do this? If once feels like it's not enough, do it a few times, but don't keep nagging the spirit with the same request. If you feel like you do it well enough to make your point then you're done, whether it's three days or twenty.

Stop asking questions. Stop worrying about why it won't work. Pick a spirit to bring you something you desire and do the magick.

Chapter 13: Making New Magick

In your career as a Magician of Chaos, you don't have to make magick up. But knowing how it's done can give you clues that help you see the real energy behind magick, which can improve all of your magick. You may never invent anything, but knowing that a combination of essential symbols, a history of belief and a simplified system can lead to success, might open you up when working magick.

Making up magick can be simple, but if it's too simple, it's not much better than crossing your fingers or making a wish. Get confident, and know that you can throw away most of the rules and regulations. But know that there comes a point when something is too simple, and then it's not really magick anymore.

When developing a system of Olympic Chaos Magick, I could have simplified it even more. The most basic sigil for Arathron looks like this:

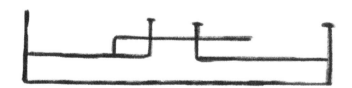

There's no circle, no magick words, and I could have said that you stare at the sigil and call out, 'Arathron, help me to...' That's it. That's classic Chaos Magick.

It might work, but I think it feels too trivial, too loose, too slapdash, and it's like too much of the original system has been tossed out. If you repeat it every night for a month, it might work. But why not put the time into developing a system that takes the essence of an ancient system, the flavor and the color, without the rules and regulations?

Here's how Olympic Chaos Magick was developed (with the help of my friends). This sort of borders on being theoretical, so I'm going to make this a **very short** explanation. *Arbatel: Of the Magic of the Ancients* was my starting point. You can find the Olympic Spirits in other books, like *The Grimoire of Turiel*, but *Arbatel* has the detail you need to get the ideas behind the magick.

With *Arbatel* in hand, I hunted down the essence of the magick. What's it actually about? At first glance, you might think it's about being pure of spirit, facing a particular direction at a particular time, and calling to a spirit. Although it's not as complex as some bizarre systems, it's still got lots of rules and lots of things you supposedly have to do. Follow *Arbatel* as it's written and you've got a load of work to do. But, when you cut away the dross, you find the spirit names, a hint of their powers, knowledge of their associated planet, their sigils, and a sense that you will need divine authority to connect to them.

I threw out the rest and used the basic ritual structure that I described earlier in the book. I also added a dash of emotional transmutation. If you read *Arbatel,* you can see that emotional transmutation fits right in. You need to read between the lines.

The sigils were redrawn from the originals, in my own hand. I added the circle and the square because the full magickal method in *Arbatel* describes a longwinded process where you draw a circle within a square. I kept the feeling of that circle-squareness and put it into the sigil. The sigil also looks a bit like one you find in *The Grimoire of Turiel*, which is used for contacting Olympic spirits. I wasn't just making something new, but blending magick from many sources. The words around the edge are *Adonai, Shaddai,* and the *Tetragrammaton*. I chose these because they were used in *The Grimoire of Turiel*; although, in that grimoire, they were written in English, with a fairly crappy transliteration. I changed that to Hebrew; it looks more magickal and feels more authentic.

But that's it. I threw out the complications and worked with the names, sigils, and powers. I made the list of powers intuitively by meditating on the names of the spirits. I trusted those lists and stuck with them. I took the bits that I liked, made it feel magickal, added emotional transmutation, and there was my homemade magick system. If you try it, you will find that it works, more or less. It wasn't made up, but it isn't traditional ceremonial magick as described in Arbatel. It's Chaos Magick.

There is a catch. The more your system is used, the better it gets... which means that the newer your system is, the less power it has. You're tapping into real power, with sigils and names that have been known for centuries. That's good. Your system may work a little bit right away, but the more it's used, the easier it becomes to get results.

There's no predicting how long this might take, because you could adjust your system – adding some things back in, taking others out. It can take weeks or years to get your system really firing on all cylinders. That homemade Olympic Magick System has been around for over eight years, frequently used by me and a few others, which makes it more workable than if I came up with it yesterday. But, don't let this put you off trying when the time comes, because you can never underestimate the power of emotional transmutation. It can bring all magick to life.

Take any old crappy spell off the internet and add emotional transmutation, and guess what... it will probably work. Burn a candle, and let your emotions change as the wax burns away (like your problem), and you might get reality to wobble the way you want. It might not work as well as an established system, but it can work. And that gives you a real feeling of power, connection, and, let's face it, awe.

What you can take away from all this is that you can break the rules. If you follow *Arbatel* as it is written, you're in for a hell of a time. It's complicated, longwinded and you're going to need a really good compass to work out which direction to face. But here's the secret – those rules mostly don't matter. If you read a wicca spell, and it says you need to collect rosehips from a south-facing hillside, you know that spell's going to feel half-baked if you just buy a jar of rosehips. But, what Chaos Magick tells you is that you don't even *need* the rosehips. You can just pretend the rosehips are there, or use something else and believe it's as good.

The structures of magick are often put there just to help get you in the mood, to build your faith, or to make things feel magickal. When you craft a ritual, make it feel magickal – keep the sounds, names and sigils that feel essential to you, and use emotional transmutation. It will work.

I doubt that you're about to dash out and buy lots of ancient grimoires and build your own system. But, I bet there will be times when you want to modify a system, and now you know how. When you see how many rules can be chucked out with the magick still being effective, it makes you a bold occultist. You stop fretting about the details and focus on the spirits you're calling. They listen. They react. They work for you.

And, as you experiment, you find that some words of power are better than others, some entities are easier to contact than others, and sometimes you do need exactly the right equipment and timing. But, most of the time you don't. You only need the essential magickal symbols and the energy of emotional transmutation. If you missed it, here's what you do:

Clear a space for magick.
(Banish, confess or let go of troubles.)

Take on magickal authority.
(Do it like you mean it.)

Get the spirit to listen.
(Use names, sigils, and words of power.)

Say what you want.
(But with feeling. Feel what you want to feel when it all works out.)

Make an offering.
(Offer gratitude, emotion or something else.)

Get back to normal.
(Work on your problem as though the magick won't work, but believe the magick will work. And the magick will work.)

That's what you do.
But only when you need to.
Or only when it's worth your while.

We made Olympic Chaos Magick because the classical approach to those particular spirits was too dreary. We really wanted to work with those qualities of the Planetary Powers in an exciting way, so we built a magick that sounded like it would work, and adjusted it until it did.

In Chaos Magick you're encouraged to experiment, make things up. Yep, good, but I want to hammer home this big time-saver: If there's a system that works in a simple way already, don't waste your time building a new one. If you own a car, don't hitchhike.

Inventing magick is cool, but not vital, even though some folks will swear this is the definition of Chaos Magick. I think invention is optional. Right now, if you want a result, I'd say use the Olympic system. It's probably going to work way better than a new system that you invent. But, when you feel the urge to invent, you've got all the clues you need.

Never be afraid to draw on traditional magick; there's so much power in what has gone before. Don't strand yourself in the details, though. Get to the essence of the magick and fill it with emotion, and simplify, but don't simplify to the point where it's too dumb or abstract to work. It may take some experimentation to find out what works, but you can simplify magick and get results. Break the rules without breaking the magick.

And if you're wondering about the magick circle, I didn't bother with one. Magick circles cannot be neglected, according to many great authorities. If you believe the great authorities, you can look up some way of drawing a circle on the floor, or in your mind, and protect yourself there, or bring the spirits to the circle, or near the circle... I get confused. I don't bother with magick circles. They take time and space and make no difference to the magick. If that makes me a heretic, so be it. This is Chaos Magick.

Chapter 14: The Magick of Pure Invention

'Duh, yeah, obviously.'

'That's nothing new.'

'What the…? It will never work unless you do the magick at the right hour, facing the right direction.'

'Why would I want to make magick up when there's already magick made up for me?'

All those thoughts are OK by me, but if you get Olympic Chaos Magick to work, then you show yourself that magick can be simplified so long as it is not simplified beyond recognition.

Hordes of folks would disagree and say that you can make up magick completely and get it to work; I can't argue with that, because it's true. Some people would also call me a second-rate Chaos Magician for relying on all that traditional ceremonial stuff.

The alternative is pure invention – make magick up and keep doing it until it works. There's a trick to this; you do the magick for something that is absolutely inevitable. You create a ritual for money magick, and then you do that ritual to get paid your weekly wage. The magick *has* to work! That makes the magick real, and after doing rituals for things that are bound to happen, you do it for things that are quite likely, and then eventually you find that your completely and utterly invented spirits are actually able to bring results. It's a lot of effort, but I have to put it out there. Chaos Magick is partly about invention, so if you want to invent, that's one way.

Another is to create thoughtforms, as described earlier, but then treat them as though they are ancient spirits rather than your own thoughtforms. Draw up a sigil, and tell your thoughtform that it can only work when you call it with a set of magick words and a ritual, and by chanting its name over the sigil. If you do that, you've sort of created a servitor, but one that thinks it's a spirit and that can be summoned by anybody who knows the system, sigil, and method you've created.

Why bother with pure invention? Because sometimes, no matter how many books you consult, there just isn't quite the entity you're looking for. You might have some area of your life that's so specific, narrow and unusual that nobody else has come up with a magickal solution. That's when you make time for the magick of pure invention.

Chapter 15: The Big Picture

Chaos Magick is a vibe. You might be thinking that I should have given better instructions, more details, or a bigger list of spirits to contact. But, Chaos Magick is a vibe, and you get the vibe. The real Master Works of Chaos Magick are the ones that you get to work for *you*. You know enough now to get it working.

When you read about Chaos Magick, you hear the word *experiment*, because this isn't dogmatic magick that plays by ancient rules. Every ritual is an experiment. But the problem with that word is that an experiment is something you do to test a theory. If you test magick as though it's a theory, it will prove that the Law of Physics and Normality are real and that magick is for lame losers. When you experiment, be like a bad scientist. Bad scientists think they know the answer before they do the experiment. That's not good for science, because the results get fudged... but it's good for magick because you expect the best. Assume that the thing's going to work, really cool and casual.

But, how do you work out what's working, and what's a waste of time? You just know. Do a ritual, and if it fires off well and gives you a return, you know your system is great. If it's not your thing, you'll get that – you'll know. You'll get a vibe, and that's enough.

There's a chaos tradition that says you should invent a banishing ritual of your own to ward off evil, or intrusive spirits, or annoying dogs, or whatever's lurking in your neighborhood. It's not a bad idea, trying this, but it's not obligatory. When you read about Chaos Magick, you'll see people saying that you really *must* create a banishing ritual and that you absolutely have to create a servitor. Like there are rules...

When The Gallery of Magick was young, we messed around with homemade banishing rituals because some of the work we'd done made the place we worked feel creepy. When the lights were out during the dark and dreary rituals, it felt a bit too weird and spooky, and like ghosts and demons were taking an interest. We came up with this really great banishing, where we all shouted, 'Bugger off,' at the same time. It worked. Then, we came up with something even easier: we turned the lights back on. When you can, you simplify.

Chaos Magick is not your annoying uncle. Remember that Uncle who told you that you *should* go into real estate, or that you *must* be better at school? Maybe not. Maybe that was just me. But, annoying relatives infamously insist that you *should* and *must*. In Chaos there is no *should* and no *must*. What I give you here is a guideline that can kick you in the right direction, but then you can do what you want. Others say you *must* meditate, you *must* join an order, you *should* work for the higher good of all. Nope. Do magick, and that is all.

Chaos Magick can be the beginning of magick – the first magick you try, where you sense the potential of the occult.

Chaos Magick can be something you come to later in life, to help you break through dogma and try new magickal technology.

Chaos Magick is not a religion, and it's only as good as the results you get.

Who knows what magick is? It might be the art and science of getting things done using the paranormal. It might be a way of reaching for the divine, knowing yourself, sensing your inner power, or something else entirely. But, magick happens, weirdly enough. It shouldn't be any more effective than throwing a coin into a wishing well – which *can* be a magickal act. Put some magickal energy into the coin. Feel your desire. Feel what you lack. As you throw the coin in, know that when it hits the water, your desire is manifest. Feel good that you have the result. Instant Wishing Well Chaos Magick. You get the idea.

Adam Blackthorne

Afterword

If you have questions, our website is an excellent source of background material and practical posts that help you to get magick working. We could have published two or three books on magickal practice, but instead, it's all there for free. You can also find extensive FAQs for every book. I urge you to make good use of the site when you encounter problems, and also when you wish to expand your understanding of magick.

There are new posts every few weeks, and they can help keep your magick vital and hone your understanding.

The Gallery of Magick Facebook page will also keep you up to date. Please note that we only have one official Facebook page, and information in various fan groups is not always accurate.

I hope you use and enjoy the sigils and talismans in this book, but please note that they are not meant to be worn as amulets, worn on the body, turned into tattoos, put up on walls or hidden in wallets. Their power comes not from being worn as jewelry or decoration, but by being used as described. As such, the only copies you make should be for personal use within your own magick. These sigils, as drawn here, are not in the public domain, so they should not be used for resale of any kind. To make personal copies, you can photocopy, photograph or take screenshots and print them out, or use them on a device or computer screen.

If you have an interest in developing your magick further, there are many texts that can assist you. *The 72 Sigils of Power* by Zanna Blaise covers Contemplation Magic (for insight and wisdom) and Results Magic (for changing the world around you). She is also the author of *The Angels of Love*, which can heal relationships and attract a soulmate.

Words of Power and *The Greater Words of Power* present an extremely simple ritual practice, for bringing about change in yourself and others, as well as directing and attracting changed circumstances.

For those seeking more money, *Magickal Cashbook* uses a

ritual to attract small bursts of money out of the blue, and works best when you are not desperate, but when you can approach the magick with a sense of enjoyment and pleasure. *Magickal Riches* is more comprehensive, with rituals for everything from gambling to sales. There is a master ritual to oversee magickal income. For the more ambitious, *Wealth Magick* contains a complex set of rituals for earning money by building a career. For those still trying to find their feet, there is *The Magickal Job Seeker*.

Magickal Protection contains rituals that can be directed at specific problems, as well as a daily practice called The Sword Banishing, which is one of our most popular and effective rituals.

For those who cannot find peace through protection, there is *Magickal Attack*, by Gordon Winterfield. Gordon has also written *Demons of Magick*, a comprehensive guide to working safely with demonic power. Dark magick is not to everybody's taste, but this is a highly moral approach that puts the emphasis on using personal sincerity. This is also exemplified in his book, *Angels of Wrath*.

The 72 Angels of Magick explores hundreds of powers that can be applied by working with these angels. *The Angels of Alchemy* works with forty-two angels for personal transformation, which can be the key to unlocking magick.

Our most successful book is *Sigils of Power and Transformation*, which has brought great results for many people. *Archangels of Magick* by Damon Brand is the most complete book of magick we have published, covering sigils, divination, invocation, and evocation.

Adam Blackthorne

www.galleryofmagick.com

Made in the USA
Las Vegas, NV
08 June 2024

90887722R00056